STEM Projects in MINECRAFT®

The Unofficial Guide to MINECRAFT® Archaeology

JILL KEPPELER

I0811749

PowerKiDS press

Published in 2025 by The Rosen Publishing Group, Inc.
2544 Clinton Street, Buffalo, NY 14224

Copyright © 2025 by The Rosen Publishing Group, Inc.

All rights reserved. No part of this book may be reproduced in any form without permission in writing from the publisher, except by a reviewer.

First Edition

Editor: Greg Roza
Book Design: Rachel Rising
Illustrator: Matias Lapegüe

Photo Credits: Cover, pp. 1, 3–24 Soloma/Shutterstock.com; pp. 4, 6, 8, 10, 12, 14, 16, 18, 20 Levent Konuk/Shutterstock.com; p. 5 Microgen/Shutterstock.com; p. 11 Roberto Sorin/Shutterstock.com; p. 11 Subbotina Anna/Shutterstock.com; p. 13 Elnur/Shutterstock.com; p. 21 SeventyFour/Shutterstock.com.

Library of Congress Cataloging-in-Publication Data

Names: Keppeler, Jill, author.
Title: The unofficial guide to Minecraft archaeology / Jill Keppeler.
Description: Buffalo, N.Y. : PowerKids Press, [2025] | Series: STEM projects in minecraft | Includes bibliographical references and index.
Identifiers: LCCN 2023056641 (print) | LCCN 2023056642 (ebook) | ISBN 9781499446937 (library binding) | ISBN 9781499446920 (paperback) | ISBN 9781499446944 (ebook)
Subjects: LCSH: Archaeology–Juvenile literature. | Minecraft (Game)–Juvenile literature.
Classification: LCC CC171 .K47 2025 (print) | LCC CC171 (ebook) | DDC 930.1–dc23/eng/20231214
LC record available at https://lccn.loc.gov/2023056641
LC ebook record available at https://lccn.loc.gov/2023056642

Minecraft is a trademark of Mojang (a game development studio owned by Microsoft Technology Corporation), and its use in this book does not imply a recommendation or endorsement of this title by Mojang or Microsoft. Manufactured in the United States of America

Some of the images in this book illustrate individuals who are models. The depictions do not imply actual situations or events.

Manufactured in the United States of America

CPSIA Compliance Information: Batch #CWPK20. For Further Information contact Rosen Publishing, New York, New York at 1-800-237-9932.

Find us on

Contents

Out of the Past

People have lived on Earth for thousands of years. Archaeology is the study of things made and left behind by people of the past. These things may be tools, art, buildings, and other items. Real-life archaeologists often work at the sites of old cities or other places where people lived. These may be called dig sites.

In *Minecraft*, players can also take part in archaeology. You can study the land around you to find special blocks, and then you can use certain tools on those blocks. What do you think you might find?

MINECRAFT MANIA

In the real-life world, archaeologists study dig sites and the things they find there to learn more about the people of the past who lived in those places. Who might have left things behind in *Minecraft*?

Archaeologists must work very slowly and carefully to uncover these pieces of the past, which are called artifacts.

Sites and Structures

To take part in archaeology, you need to look for places that look like past people might have built them. This is also true in a *Minecraft* world. There are many structures that **generate** when a world does. Part of the fun of the game can be finding and exploring these features.

However, not all *Minecraft* structures or features can be archaeological dig sites. As a would-be archaeologist, you'll want to look for warm or cold ocean ruins, desert **pyramids**, desert ruins, and trail ruins. These places are where you can **excavate** treasures like those you would find at a real-world dig site.

MINECRAFT MANIA

Other *Minecraft* sites and structures include abandoned villages, **ancient** cities deep underground, jungle temples, and shipwrecks. All may have loot or other items hidden in chests.

A desert well will have suspicious sand underneath the water source block in the center.

Ocean ruins usually are found deep under the surface of the water in *Minecraft*. They might have one building or many. Cold ocean ruins are made mostly of stone bricks, while warm ocean ruins are made mostly of sandstone.

Desert pyramids are big structures with several rooms. They're made mostly of sandstone. So are desert wells, which are much smaller structures with a water source inside. Trail ruins are structures with a main road and several buildings. Players can find them in **biomes** with many trees. Some trail ruins may have only the top of one tower unburied.

MINECRAFT MANIA

Minecraft has a few different types of ocean biomes. You can tell if an ocean biome is warm, lukewarm, or cold depending on its water color and plant and animal life.

If you want to go underwater to find an ocean ruin, you'll need a way to breathe there. A potion of water breathing is one way to do so.

What's in There?

There's one important thing that makes the previously mentioned sites and structures subjects for *Minecraft* archaeology. This is the presence of suspicious sand or suspicious gravel. These blocks are very like regular *Minecraft* sand or gravel but have a slightly different **texture**. There are bigger, darker spots on their surface.

Players can find these blocks in different places at the different sites. Suspicious sand will generate in buried rooms in desert pyramids, in desert wells, and in warm ocean ruins. Suspicious gravel will generate in trail ruins and cold ocean ruins.

MINECRAFT MANIA

Like regular sand and gravel (and unlike most other *Minecraft* blocks), suspicious sand and gravel blocks are subject to gravity. They'll break and drop nothing if they fall.

In a desert pyramid, enter the main room, shown, which has a pattern of colored terracotta in the middle. Look for blocks of sand in the floor instead of sandstone. Dig down into this sand and keep an eye out for more terracotta and suspicious sand!

Tools of the Trade

Suspicious sand and gravel can hold special items, but players need the right tool to remove them. While shovels or other *Minecraft* tools can break these blocks quickly, they won't drop anything if broken. Instead, you must use a brush to clean the sand or gravel away—just like archaeologists in real life.

To make a brush, combine a feather, a stick, and a copper **ingot** while using a *Minecraft* crafting table. If a player uses the brush on suspicious sand or gravel, the block will begin to crack, **particles** will appear in the air, and an item will begin to emerge.

MINECRAFT MANIA

After a block of suspicious sand or gravel drops any item it holds, the block turns into regular sand or gravel.

Real-life archaeologists use brushes to uncover small parts of artifacts. They also use many other tools.

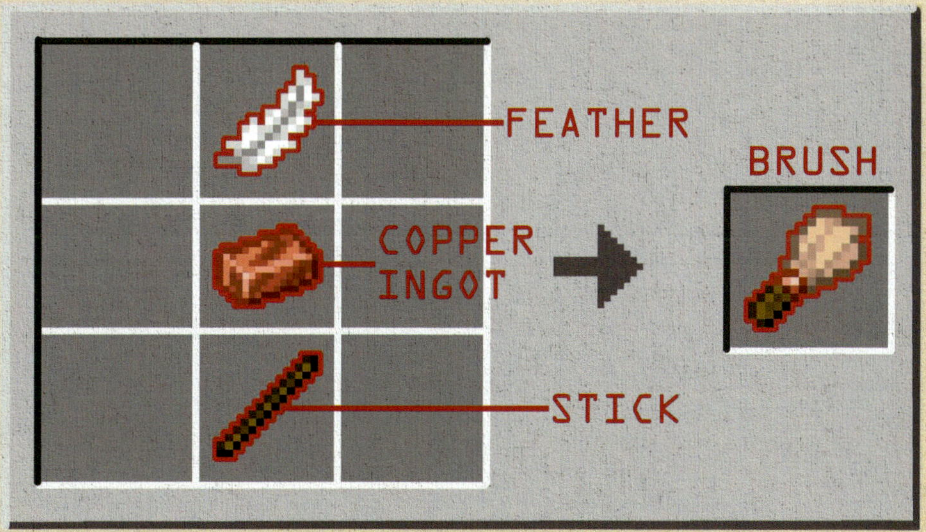

Looking for Loot

So, you've found an archaeology site in *Minecraft*. You've crafted a brush and used it on suspicious sand or gravel. What might you find? This will depend in part on what sort of site you found. Different sites have different loot.

You might find items such as **dye**, candles, tools, bricks, stained glass, or seeds. You might find gemstones such as emeralds or diamonds. In rarer cases, you can find a special music **disc** (called "relic" and only found in trail ruins), pottery sherds, armor trim smithing **templates**, or even a sniffer egg.

MINECRAFT MANIA

Players can use armor trim smithing templates and a smithing table to put decoration on their armor. There are 16 kinds of trims.

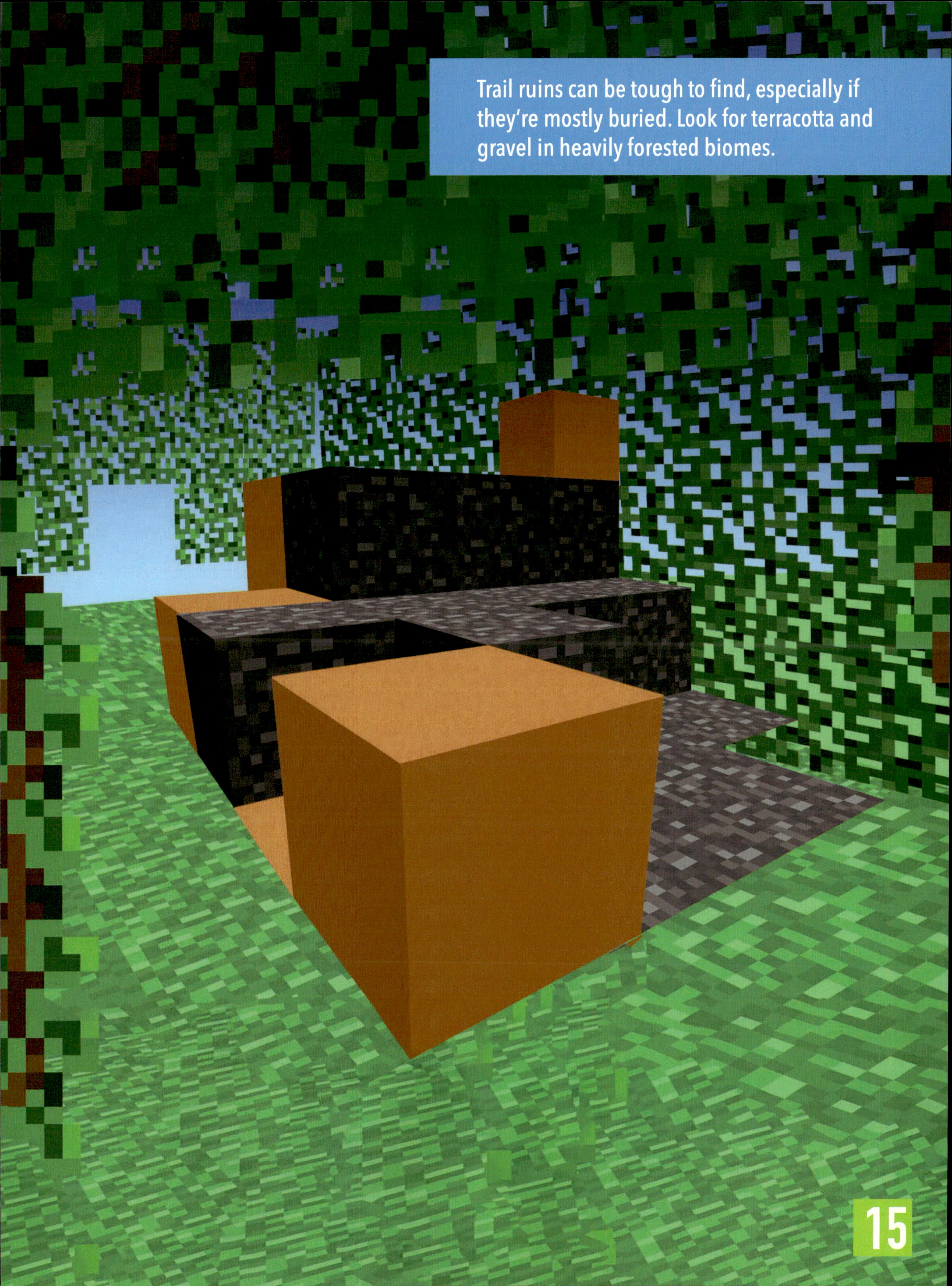

Trail ruins can be tough to find, especially if they're mostly buried. Look for terracotta and gravel in heavily forested biomes.

Sherd About This?

It's easy to misread "pottery sherds" as "pottery shards." A shard is a piece of something breakable. A sherd, however, is a piece of a pottery vessel that was found at an archaeological site. In *Minecraft*, pottery sherds are small, brown pieces of pottery that you can only find in suspicious sand or gravel.

There are 20 types of pottery sherds in the game, each with a different pattern. You can find different ones in different structures. Players can use four pottery sherds (or four bricks) to make a decorated pot. If pottery sherds are used, the pot will have the pattern of the sherds on its sides.

MINECRAFT MANIA

The makers of *Minecraft* actually changed the name of pottery sherds after real archaeologists told them that "shards" was the wrong word.

This image shows some of the patterns you can create on decorated pots in *Minecraft*.

Seeking Sniffers

One of the rarest things you can find in suspicious sand is a sniffer egg. This item can only be found in warm ocean ruins. Sniffer eggs are brown with green spots. If you place them on a block and wait, a snifflet, or baby sniffer, will hatch in time! A snifflet grows up to be a sniffer.

Sniffers are a **unique** *Minecraft* mob. They're brown and green and look shaggy. They wander around and sniff things. Sometimes, they'll stop and dig into the ground, coming up with torchflower seeds or a pitcher pod. This is the only way to get these seeds in the game.

MINECRAFT MANIA

Sniffer eggs hatch faster when placed on moss blocks. You can get moss in lush caves biomes.

This sniffer is searching for seeds on a hilltop forest biome.

Learning More

Real-life archaeologists try to understand more about the past people who used the objects they find. Who left the objects you find through archaeology in *Minecraft*? Maybe it was long-ago villagers who created the game's ancient cities. Maybe it was mobs or characters we haven't seen in the game yet! Someday, perhaps the *Minecraft* creators will let us know.

Even though we're not sure yet, you can still learn about the ideas behind archaeology by practicing this science in *Minecraft*. You can seek out the ruins left behind, hunt for dig sites, and carefully uncover special objects. Who knows what you'll learn in the future!

MINECRAFT MANIA

Minecraft's ancient cities are only found in deep dark biomes far beneath the surface. There's no suspicious sand or gravel (yet), but you can find chests full of unique loot.

If you want to be an archaeologist in real life, study science and history. You could discover many things!

Glossary

ancient: Very old.

biome: A natural community of plants and animals, such as a forest or desert.

disc: A flat, thin, round item. A music disc in *Minecraft* is something that can be played in a jukebox block.

dye: Something used to change the color of something else.

excavate: To uncover something by digging away and removing the earth that covers it.

generate: To cause to be created.

ingot: A solid piece of metal formed into a brick.

particle: A very small bit of matter.

pyramid: A structure that's wide near the bottom and narrows as it reaches the top.

template: A pattern that can be used to make the same shape or pattern in something else.

texture: The way something feels when you touch it. In images and games, the way something looks like it would feel if you could touch it.

unique: Special or different from anything else.

For More Information

BOOKS

Mojang AB and the Official Minecraft Team. *Minecraft Guide to Exploration.* New York, NY: Random House Worlds, 2023.

Romero, Libby. *National Geographic Readers: What Is an Archaeologist?* Washington, D.C.: National Geographic Kids, 2019.

Sockin, Caitlin. *Dig It! Archaeology for Kids.* Cary, NC: Persnickety Press, 2023.

WEBSITES

Archaeology Coming to Minecraft
www.minecraft.net/en-us/article/archeology-coming-minecraft-120
The official *Minecraft* site talks about the introduction of archaeology.

Archaeology for Kids
www.nps.gov/subjects/archeology/archeology-for-kids.htm
The National Parks Service offers advice on visiting archaeological sites yourself.

What Is Archaeology?
www.amnh.org/explore/ology/archaeology
The American Museum of Natural History discusses this science.

Publisher's note to educators and parents: Our editors have carefully reviewed these websites to ensure that they are suitable for students. Many websites change frequently, however, and we cannot guarantee that a site's future contents will continue to meet our high standards of quality and educational value. Be advised that students should be closely supervised whenever they access the internet.

Index